A SHORT TALE OF TAILS

Balboa Press books may be ordered through booksellers or by contacting:

Balboa Press
A Division of Hay House
1663 Liberty Drive
Bloomington, IN 47403
www.balboapress.com
1 (877) 407-4847

Because of the dynamic nature of the Internet, any web addresses or links contained in this book may have changed since publication and may no longer be valid. The views expressed in this work are solely those of the author and do not necessarily reflect the views of the publisher, and the publisher hereby disclaims any responsibility for them.

ISBN: 978-1-9822-4966-3 (sc)
ISBN: 978-1-9822-4967-0 (e)

Print information available on the last page.

Balboa Press rev. date: 07/13/2020

BALBOA.PRESS
A DIVISION OF HAY HOUSE

A SHORT TALE OF TAILS

WRITTEN AND ILLUSTRATED BY: LATONYA D. GIST

This book is dedicated to my
grandchildren:

Malik

Malakhi

Amia

Aleah

Nia-Skyy

Sarah-Santi

Khali Rose

BLUE WHALES

THE BLUE WHALE IS THE LARGEST KNOWN CREATURE ON EARTH

THE BABY WHALE CAN WEIGHT UP TO 6000 POUNDS AT BIRTH

WHALES ARE THE SIZE OF TWO SCHOOL BUSES

OR A PROFESSIONAL BASKETBALL COURT

THEY HAVE TWO NOSTRILS OPENINGS CALLED 'BLOWHOLES'

WHERE WATER COMES THROUGH SIMILAR TO A SNORT

WHALES CAN LIVE UP TO 90 YEARS OR MORE IN AN OPEN OCEAN

WATER COMES THROUGH THEIR NOSE LIKE A MILD EXPLOSION

ELEPHANTS

ELEPHANTS ARE THE LARGEST LAND MAMMALS KNOWN
THE JUNGLE OR RAINFOREST IS WHERE
THEY WOULD LIKE TO CALL HOME

ELEPHANTS ARE KNOWN TO HAVE A GOOD MEMORY
THEY ARE VERY SMART, SOCIABLE, AND WHEN HAPPY
OR SAD THEY CAN BE VERY EMOTIONAL.

THEIR EARS CAN REACH UP TO FIVE FEET LONG
THEY LIKE BONDING WITH THEIR FAMILY AND
FRIENDS AND DON'T LIKE BEING ALONG

ELEPHANTS SPEND 12 TO 18 HOURS EATING
THEY LIKE GRASS, BARK, FRUIT, AND TWIGS
THAT'S PROBABLY HOW THEY GET SO BIG!

ORANGUTAN

I'M A BROWNISH RED ORANGUTAN

YOU CAN FIND ME IN THE RAINFOREST
THAT'S WHERE I LIKE TO HANG.

I SEARCH FOR FOOD MOST OF THE DAY
MY ARMS ARE LONGER THAN MY LEGS I MUST SAY

EACH NIGHT I BUILD A NEST BEFORE I GO TO SLEEP
AND COVER MYSELF FROM MY HEAD TO MY FEET

 COWS

I'M A BLACK AND WHITE COW

I EAT GRASS AND HAY

I ALSO GIVE AND PRODUCE MILK

TO DRINK WITH YOUR BREAKFAST EVERYDAY

HIPPOPOTAMUS

I'M A HIPPOPOTAMUS AND I'M ALSO CALLED A HIPPO

I'M THE SECOND LARGEST MAMMAL ON EARTH

THE ELEPHANT IS THE FIRST

MY EYES, EARS, AND NOSE ARE LOCATED ON THE TOP OF MY HEAD

FALLING FRUIT AND GRASS IS WHAT I'M FED

MY SKIN SWEAT AN OILY FLUID AND THE COLOR IS RED

TO STAY COOL IN AFRICA FROM THE HOT HEAT

I SPEND MOST OF THE DAY IN RIVERS AND LAKES RESTING MY FEET

LIONS

I COULD WEIGHT ALMOST 500 POUNDS

AND LEAP 40 FEET IN THE AIR

WITH THE WIND BLOWING THROUGH MY GOLDEN BROWN HAIR

LIONS ARE THE LAZIEST OF ALL THE BIG CATS,

AND SLEEP UP TO 16 HOURS IN A DAY

THEIR ROAR IS SO LOUD IT COULD BE HEARD UP TO 5 MILES AWAY!

LIONS ARE NOT THE GREATEST WHEN IT COME TO CLIMBING TREE'S

I MARK MY TERRITORY WITH A SCENT OF ME

(HOLD YOUR NOSE)

POLAR BEAR

I'M A POLAR BEAR

WHITE IS THE COLOR OF MY FURRY HAIR

I LOVE THE COLD SNOW FLURRIES IN THE AIR

THE ARCTIC CIRCLE OF THE NORTH POLE IS WHERE I CAN BE FOUND

MY WEIGHT CAN BE AS BIG AS 1700 POUNDS

I'M AN EXCELLENT SWIMMER

MY FOOD OF CHOICE IS SEALS

I WAIT FOR THEM TO COME TO SURFACE

THEN I CAN HAVE MY MEAL

ZEBRA

I'M A ZEBRA, I CAME FROM AFRICA

I LIKE TO RUN AROUND THE GREEN PASTURES

WHERE I EAT A LOT OF GRASS

I CAN RUN UP TO 35MPH!! NOW THAT'S FAST!!

THERE ARE NO TWO ZEBRA'S STRIPES THE SAME

WE ALL HAVE UNIQUE BLACK AND WHITE STRIPES

I HAVE A GOOD EYESIGHT, ESPECIALLY AT NIGHT

THEREFORE, IF DANGER COME I WILL SEE, AND

KICK WITH MY STRONG LEGS AND FIGHT!

I WILL THEN RUN WITH ALL MY MIGHT!!

BEAR

I'M A BIG BROWN BEAR

I STAY IN HIBERNATION WHICH MEAN SLEEP

FOR MAYBE 6 WINTER MONTHS

WHEN I WAKE UP IN THE SPRING

I WILL BE READY FOR MY LUNCH

I GET MY FOOD THAT I KEEP STORED IN A HOLE

I EAT IT ALL WITHOUT A BOWL

MONKEYS

MONKEYS CAN WALK ACROSS A TREE TOP
AND USE THEIR LEGS TO SWING
MONKEYS LONG ARMS AND LEGS ARE FLEXIBLE
AND CAN SWING ON ALMOST EVERYTHING.

MONKEYS LIVE IN TREE'S AND SOME ON THE GROUND
THEY CAN BE VERY NOISY, MAKING LOUD POUNDING SOUNDS

MONKEY'S ARE SO LOUD THEY CAN BE HEARD A MILE AWAY
WHETHER THEY'RE BEING NAUGHTY OR JUST AT PLAY

MONKEY'S ARE SNEAKY AND SMART
YET CUTE AND SOCIAL AND CAN WIN YOUR HEART

NOW LOOK! YOU CAN'T FULLY TRUST THEM
THEY WILL STEAL YOUR FOOD

BEFORE YOU KNOW IT...
IT WILL ALL BE CHEWED
NOW ISN'T THAT RUDE!

PIG

I'M A PIG AND MY EYESIGHT IS NOT SO GOOD

I WOULD WEAR EYE GLASSES IF I COULD

I HAVE A SKIN TONE OF PINK

I'M SMARTER THAN YOU THINK

I HAVE A BIG SNOUT YOU MAY CALL A NOSE

AND A GOOD SENSE OF SMELL

I HAVE BIG FLAPPY EARS CAN ALSO HEAR VERY WELL

TO STAY COOL I LIKE TO WADDLE IN THE MUD

AND I HAVE OVER 5000 TASTE BUDS

GIRAFFE

THE GIRAFFE IS THE TALLEST MAMMAL ON EARTH
THE BABY GIRAFFE CAN EVEN STAND AN HOUR AFTER BIRTH

GIRAFFES LIKE TO LIVE IN CLIMATES THAT IS DRY AND HOTTER
AND CAN SURVIVE 2 TO 3 DAYS WITHOUT DRINKING WATER
THEIR LONG LEGS MAKE IT DIFFICULT TO TAKE A SQUATTER

GIRAFFES SPEND MOST OF THE DAY STANDING UP AND
REQUIRES A 5 TO 30 MINUTES OF SLEEP A DAY
THEIR LONG LEGS MAKE IT DIFFICULT TO SIT OR LAY

TIGERS

TIGERS CAN LIVE 10 TO 26 YEARS MAYBE MORE IN THE WILD
THEY CAN WEIGHT 240 TO 670 POUNDS

TIGERS ARE ORANGE TONES WITH STUNNING STRIPES
THE BENGAL TIGER IS DIFFERENT
IT IS WHITE WITH STRIPES

TIGERS HAVE AN EXCELLENT EYESIGHT
THEIR VISION IS 6 TIMES GREATER AT NIGHT

THAT'S WHY THEY WAIT TIL DARK TO HUNT
THEY THEN LOOK FOR BREAKFAST, DINNER, AND LUNCH

TIGERS ARE POWERFUL SWIMMERS
THEY ARE CAPABLE OF SWIMMING IN LAKES AND RIVERS

TIGERS MARK THEIR TERRITORY WITH
SPECIAL SCRATCHES ON TREES
CONSTANTLY PATROLLING THEIR AREA WITH THEIR STINKY PEE

Printed in the United States
By Bookmasters